Dare to Dink!

Pickleball for Seniors

and Anyone Else Who Wants to Have Fun

Sally Huss

Copyright © 2021 Sally Huss
All rights reserved.
ISBN: 9781945742675

Preface

    I love pickleball, but I must confess that I am not an expert pickleball player, nor am I an expert pickleball instructor. I am, however, someone who has hit a lot of balls, tennis balls specifically, and who has now put her toe into this new craze called **PICKLEBALL**. I encourage you to join me, if you have not already. Here I will pass on some of the basics for playing this game, some of the most notable benefits, and even some of the underlying delights that this fine activity offers.

    I also must warn you that pickleball is addictive. I will go into that later.

History

The game of pickleball started in the summer of 1965, although you may not have heard of it until now. It was originally created as a children's backyard game, then through its popularity, spread to community centers, physical education classes, public parks, private health clubs, YMCA facilities, and retirement communities. Not surprisingly, now there are local, national and international championships held throughout the world. The possibility of including it in Olympic competition is looming.

"The hardest part about playing pickleball is learning the names of all of my new friends!"
-- Pat Treacy, age 80, 3.5 level

There seems to be some confusion as to the origin of the name "pickleball." Joan Pritchard, wife of one of the creators of the game set it right, according to Wikipedia, by saying that "The name of the game became "Pickle Ball" after I said it reminded me of the Pickle Boat in crew where oarsmen were chosen from the leftovers of other boats." Later Pritchard's dog Pickles was named for the game and not the other way round, as many believe. Either way, this is what this book is about.

My History

I first heard the word "pickleball" when some of my tennis friends in La Jolla, California would leave the tennis court after a match and with big smiles on their faces head to the beach where someone had set up a pickleball court. I stayed on the tennis court.

Next, when we moved to Colorado, the tennis pro at the Country Club of Colorado Springs Steve Campbell and I would snicker when the word "pickleball" was mentioned. With our noses in the air, we both agreed that it was definitely a "game" and not a "sport." After all, I had spent nearly my entire life on a tennis court. As a tennis champion (National and Wimbledon Junior Champion, semi-finalist in the Women's Division at Wimbledon, and later one of the top senior players in the world), why would I want to legitimize this activity? Beyond that, why would I ever want to start over in another game/sport at the age of 81?

Then, we moved to a charming neighborhood in Colorado Springs called Pleasant Valley. The "hood", as the locals call it, has its own park. It's nothing fancy, but it does have two tennis courts. These are tennis courts in name only. They resemble street pavement with cracks and weeds growing out of the cracks. It was there that I hit my first pickleball.

I had noticed there was a group of women of various ages who inhabited these courts on a regular basis with paddles and whiffle balls. A couple of fellows were sprinkled in too. I dared to observe their play one afternoon and looked longingly like I wanted to join in. The truth is I just wanted to make new friends. When one player had enough, I was invited in. There was no problem that I had never played before, they weren't very good themselves and they really didn't know the scoring or rules. But, they were having fun.

"Nothing has expanded and strengthened the friendships in my life like pickleball."
-- Curt Olson, age 58, 4.5 level

I became a regular with this group that consisted at various times of Sandy, Mitzi, Greg Jeanie, Judith, Russ, Estee, Barb, Mary and Fisher, plus at least three dogs off leashes and four or five kids on bikes or skates. We worked around it all.

Occasionally, an outsider would join in who knew more than we did and our rules would change. Scoring was modified as we received more information. All those elements, including Thor's ambling across the court during play didn't bother any of us. It seemed to add color to the occasion. The balls hitting cracks, the weird strokes, the wiffing of a ball or two gave us the excuse to break into laughter. Nobody was any good and nobody cared. We called it "tickleball."

Our horizons broadened as we honed our skills. I use the word "skills" generously. We hit the wiffle ball anyway we could as anyone would who had no instruction.

Some of us ventured out to the local, authentic pickleball venues. These were public parks that had rows and rows of real pickleball courts. Our courts were tennis courts that had a few appropriate lines added to mark off the pickleball boundaries. I had not accompanied anyone on any of these outings, but I had heard. Our players' eyes were opened. They came back understanding that there were very definite levels of play and players. Some were very competitive and some more social. More impressive, all players seemed to know how to keep score and where their place was on the court. These were things we had ad-libbed.

At about this time, I had been added to the tennis teaching team at the Garden of the Gods Resort and Club where our son teaches tennis. I had been brought on to teach my particular kind of relaxed tennis called "Zennis." It is a way of playing that I had discovered through some dance work I had done years before. I had even taken it on the road as a member of the Virginia Slims Pro Tour. It was fun. It was happy. It was powerful.

Then, the Garden of the Gods Director of Racquet Sports, Scott Leifer, suggested that I learn a bit of pickleball as they needed another teacher. Scott had brought pickleball to GOG back in 2014. Naturally, I was up for it because now I had a taste of this game and was no longer so uppity about it. So, I became an assistant to the regular pickleball pro Mike Lovato, an exceptionally fine player and teacher.

I watched. I learned. I took what I had been taught back to my park gals. They were only moderately interested in improving. I was always interested in improving.

At one point, Mike had to go out of town and asked me to take over one of his classes. Petrified, still I jumped in. It wasn't hard at all. People just wanted to learn the basics. That was good because that's about all I knew. I had no history in this game/sport. I had never really played it with anyone
very accomplished. Then again, no one has a

particularly long history playing it. It's that new to the general public.

From there, I've ventured out of my local park-play comfort zone and have delved into two of the outstanding pickleball locations here in Colorado Springs: Monument Valley Park and Bear Creek Park. Bear Creek had taken out some of its tennis courts and filled the area and much more with pickleball courts.

At either of these sites, I found that a person could just arrive, survey the play, find an appropriate level, and ask to be included when there was an opening. And, there always seemed be an opening. The other players made sure of it.

With this activity, my game has improved considerably, as has my teaching, my stamina, my joie de vive, and my circle of friends.

I invite you to follow along as I explain what you need to know, how this game/sport is played, and what you will gain by putting your own toe into what is called **PICKLEBALL**!

"Happy days are made by happy people. Happy people play pickleball!"

What You Need to Know

The first thing you need to know is that anybody can play pickleball. If you can stand, you can play it. If you're in a wheelchair, you can play it. There is no excuse for not playing it, unless of course, if you are unsighted. However, once I did play with a fellow who only had one eye. On the court next to us, a woman was playing with one arm in a sling.

There are no age limitations, height limitations, weight limitations, or gender limitations. There are no economic limitations as there are in many sports. Golf is pricey. Tennis can be pricey too. But, the only pickleball requirements are a simple paddle, a wiffle ball or two, and a pair of sneakers. And it can all be played free on a public park court near you.

The uniform is whatever is in your closet that is comfortable and allows you to move freely. A hat is suggested, if you will be playing outdoors.

If you are a tennis player or have been a tennis player in the past, or a badminton, racquetball, squash or ping pong player – all the better for you in playing pickleball. But, it is not essential. Tennis strokes generally need to be shortened. Racquetball and squash players will find the speed they are used to will serve them well in pickleball. Even the skills learned on a ping pong table can be useful. If none of these applies to you, you can still learn to play pickleball.

I have seen people who have absolutely no athletic ability at all play this game well and enjoy it immensely. All it takes is a desire to do so. Therefore, if you are up for fun, this game is for you!

"Why I love pickleball? Fun, exercise, and how can you possibly take something called 'pickleball' seriously? Lots of laughs with non-competitive friends."
-- Carolyn W. Fox, age 64, 2.5 level on a good day

The Ball

Pickleball starts with the ball. It is a plastic, hollow ball with holes in it, a bit bigger than a tennis ball. It is usually yellow. In essence, it is a child's wiffle ball.

Unlike a golf ball, tennis ball, squash ball, or racquetball ball, it is unlikely that you can get hurt if you are hit with it in a social game. Naturally, in highly competitive matches with accomplished players, there is the possibility of a bruise or two if a player is hit.

"I had to retire from basketball and volleyball because of rotator cuff and back issues so I tried biking and hiking/walking to keep active, but it was just not satisfying. I needed some sport, any sport that included a ball. I heard about pickleball and thought it was worth a shot, but I was skeptical. It didn`t take long before I was hooked. Feels good to be passionate about a sport again."
-- Greg McGannon, age 63, 3.5-4.0 level

The Court

There are two kinds of pickleball courts at this time. One is a proper pickleball court, created from the ground up. The other is a converted tennis court, using tape or other means to define the boundaries of a pickleball court. Both are equally legitimate and entertaining by having the same dimensions and spaces. A pickleball court is about half the size of a tennis court.

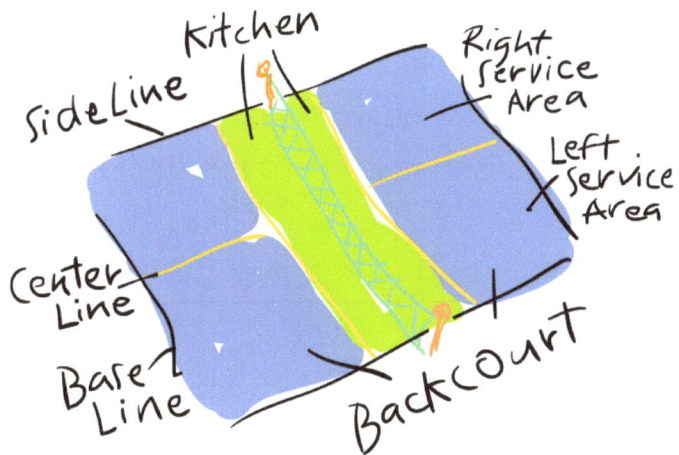

The net is slightly lower than a tennis net and divides the two sides. Next to the net on both sides of the court is the infamous "**KITCHEN.**" It is also referred to as "the no-volley zone." Why? I can't say because you can actually volley in that area by reaching into it as long as you don't step into it and volley. I prefer to call it "the kitchen." It's more whimsical. Either way, it is designated by a line (like the service line on a tennis court), however the line is considered part of the kitchen. On other courts, the kitchen is a blocked out area of color with no line. The activity at and in the kitchen determines most everything in pickleball. Just as in a normal home, the kitchen is where all delicious things happen. Everyone wants to get to the kitchen. Points are won there and strategies are tested.

The area on both sides of the court behind the kitchen is called the backcourt. It is an area that needs to be mastered well enough so that the player receiving a serve may find his or her way to the kitchen as quickly as possible. The serving player, in turn, must master the serve well enough to do the same. This backcourt area involves serving and returning serves. Tennis players and racquetball players who venture into pickleball love this area because they can incorporate their already-learned groundstrokes. But this is merely a brief thrill, as they must leave the backcourt and dash forward to the kitchen.

"It's so much fun to meet people everywhere I go and call these people my friends."
     -- Nikki King, age 63, 4.0 level

The Kitchen

The kitchen holds all the power. It is not a place for tea and crumpets. It is a place to win points and hopefully not lose friends. It is a place to move your opponent or opponents around until you have a perfect set-up to put the ball away. It also has a rule: you may not step into the kitchen to hit a ball in the air. It must bounce first.

There is one less-advertised situation regarding the kitchen. If you are standing in the kitchen or have stepped into it to retrieve a ball, your opponent may just wind up and hit you with the ball. This is also a tactic that can be used out of the kitchen. Not the kindest gesture to be sure, however, you are allowed to do the same to your opponent. So, it behooves you to only step into the kitchen to hit a ball that bounces, then step back out of the kitchen as quickly as possible, unless you get into a delightful dink rally with your opponent or opponents.

The kitchen is where you must **DARE TO DINK!** Dink, dink, dink. This is the name of the game at the kitchen. Dink into the kitchen and around the kitchen. Dump the ball over the net softly and carefully until you or your opponent accidently offers it up a bit too high and a killer shot is made. It's about sowing and reaping. Dink to sow in the hopes of reaping. **PATIENCE** is required. Actually, patience is a highly underestimated virtue in pickleball, as it is in life. So remember, when in doubt dink and patiently wait your turn to receive a set-up to slam.

At this moment, the point is usually over. But wait! There is the **VOLLEY!** Not all shots in and around the kitchen are won by first-effort put-aways. Fast hands, blocked shots back and forth across the net can save a point and prolong a rally. It is the real thrill of the game. It also reveals the essence of the game – **SPEED!** All movements and actions in pickleball, from strokes to footwork, are based on the need for speed! That is, the way you stand on the court, the way you hold the paddle, the stroke you use for any and all shots, and even the impetus to head to the kitchen are for the purpose of speed. What makes the ball go faster? What makes your reactions faster? How do you slow down an opponent so that you can quickly take advantage of a situation?

Now, do not let this emphasis on speed deter you from playing. It simply means that you must make the way you move and the way you swing the paddle at a ball as efficient as possible. The more you play, the better you get and the quicker you become – not only around the court, but also in hitting the ball. How you actually do this will be explained as we move along.

This is one thing that I really love about pickleball: it is something at which you can improve and definitely will at any age, even at my age.

"My partner Josie and I moved from Boston to Colorado Springs, but missed our friends and activities. Pickleball gave us a community. We have given up our golf clubs and bowling balls, and dust has accumulated on our tennis rackets!"
-- Helen "Boston" McChesney, age 68, 4.0 level

The Score

Probably the most difficult part of learning to play pickleball is keeping score. This is a challenge to most everyone at first, except for accountant types. So, be patient with yourself and others when errors occur. Everyone goes through a learning curve regarding score-keeping. And, everyone else is quick to set you right when you get it wrong.

Keep in mind that pickleball can be played as a singles match with two players or as a doubles match with four players. Seniors usually play doubles. So we will stick with that.

Like most ball sports, there is a serving team and a receiving team. But only the serving team can score points and that team's score is always called out first, even if it is "Zero." The second number to be called is the receiving team's score, even if it is "Zero."

For example, if Team A wins a point. The score is 1-Zero. Wait! That's not all to the score. Now we have to keep track of the serving team's players. The first server on a team serves cross-court from the right side of the court to the opponent's right side court. So, the actual score is 1-Zero-1. This last number is sometimes called out as the first server ("I'm the first server" or "I'm server Number 1"). Happy to have won a point, the first server and partner on Team A switch places. Server Number 1 continues by serving into the left side of the opposite court. Too bad! The point is lost. Now It's Server Number 2's turn. This is the other player or second player on the serving team. The score is still the same except for the last digit. Now it is 1-Zero-2.

If the serving team, Team A, wins the next point, the score is 2-Zero-2. Once again, the serving team's players switch sides and Server Number 2 serves again. This pattern continues until this serving team loses a point and ends that rotation.

Now, it is Team B's turn to serve and accrue points, if they can. Each of that team's players takes a turn at serving. The first player on this team serves from the right court to the opposite right court. That player now is Player Number 1. If this team wins a point, the score is "1-2-1." The last "1" represents the server. The "2" signifies the receiving team's points.

There is one more oddity to the scoring that you need to know. It is that the first serving team in the very beginning of a game only gets to have one server in that rotation. That player serves from the right side to the opposite right side. No second server at the beginning of play. So, the score to start things off is actually "Zero–Zero–2!" There is no apparent reason for this. You just have to accept it and play on.

Simple! However you can understand the necessity to verbally call out the score. It can be very confusing to keep things straight, even for accomplished players. Therefore, the server calls out every score before each point is played. That gives everyone else a chance to make a correction, if needed.

Points are gathered until one team wins 11 points. If the score reaches 10-All, play continues until one team succeeds in leading by two points to actually win the "game." Winning two out of three games determines the winner of a match!

This scoring system is a bit complicated but extremely beneficial for exercising your brain. That's the smartest way to look at it. Once you've mastered the scoring system, the rest of the game is a piece of cake.

"I love pickleball because of all the different people that I meet and enjoy who have this sport in common. Also, it is great exercise and good for the brain!"
-- *Susan* Brelsford, age 73, 2.5 level

Where to Go

If you like to dance, you'll love pickleball. With four players on a court, and a small court at that, there are specific moves to make with your feet and specific spaces to occupy at different times. It's better to know them than not. The reasons for making these moves have been proven by millions of players in the past and present. So, we will take their expertise as a guide to perform these dance movements around the court.

Everyone has a starting position. The server must stand behind the baseline to serve. The server's partner stays deep too. The receiver may stand anywhere, but must let the ball bounce in the proper section of the court, beyond the kitchen, before hitting it. At the same time, the receiver's partner plants his or her toes close to the edge of the kitchen and somewhere in the middle of that half of their side of the court – better to be a little toward the center.

Remember, everyone wants to get to the kitchen, not in the kitchen, but to its edge. The receiver generally wants to hit the service return deep to the serving team in order to keep the server and partner from reaching the kitchen first. It's a selfish game in this respect.

"What I love about pickleball is it's like I get to be a kid again!"
-- Mic Davis, age 69, 4.0 level

Once the return has been hit, that receiver dashes, ambles, or motors to the kitchen as quickly as possible – joining his or her partner there.

Keep in mind that you are not obliged to stay on your half of the court. You may reach over onto your partner's half and pounce on any short ball, other than a serve, that you can put away, or one your partner

may not reach in time. It's called **poaching**. Being aggressive in a controlled way is more than acceptable. Hopefully, your partner senses your move
and quickly crosses behind you to cover the court you have left open.

When it is the other team's turn to serve, the server and partner must now find their way to the kitchen as well. But wait! There is a little hitch in their get-along. The ball must bounce once on their side of the court before either can hit it back! No volleying on the way to the kitchen for the serving team. This forces one of the two serving team players to hit the dreaded **Third-Shot-Drop**! This requires a skill beyond imagining.

"Pickleball keeps me physically active and I meet wonderful friends."
               -- Lynn Coulter, age 72, 4.0 level

The Third-Shot-Drop

To hit a ball somewhere from the backcourt, as usually happens, have it clear the net and land at the feet of one of the two players at "net" (the kitchen) seems like an impossible task. It can be done. A little practice and a lot balls eaten from missed attempts will bring the importance of learning this shot to light.

You'll get it! We all do eventually. It just requires

patience, persistence, and great touch. No one is born with this ability.

Net Action

Back to dancing. There is a particular stance a player must take to be able to function efficiently and successfully at net (the kitchen). To start, stand feet a bit apart , and then bend your knees, please.

This is a crab-like shuffle, left and right, to handle all of those pesky dinks. The reason of course, like all reasons in pickleball, is that it increases your ability to deal with speed. If you were to step across your body to hit a shot, as in tennis, you would be too late to hit the returning shot. And most likely it will return! **Play as if every shot is coming back**. That way you won't be surprised when it does. Shuffle laterally, left and right, with a short step forward or back when needed with a lunge or two for wide shots and you've mastered this movement. An open stance and an open heart are all you need at net. Well, not exactly.

"Pickleball is fun, very doable, easy to learn, good exercise, and social. It's good for the brain, hand-eye coordination, and reflexes… and it's friendly."
-- Lynn Waite, age 79, 2.5 level

Competition

Another one of the unusual features of pickleball is that you can play it as non-competitively or as competitively as you like. Some players simply enjoy the exercise and the social aspects of the game and could care less about winning a match. Others thrive on the competitive opportunities the game offers. The truth is that the more you play, the better you get. And, the better you get, the more you want to play competitively. A competitive spirit can creep into an otherwise non-competitive person. Playing the game to win adds a whole dimension to the action – energy! Fortunately, the game offers all levels of play with ratings from 1.0 to 6.0+. The ratings refer to skill levels and are used for beginners up to professional pickleball players.

How to Use the Paddle

The paddle can be used in a number of ways. If you go to any pickleball location in your area, you will see that this is true. So, it might be smart to start with simple, easy-to-learn strokes that can be altered as skills are mastered. It is often hard to change an awkward or inappropriate motion once it has been imbedded in your muscle memory. Therefore, I'll offer up the simplest motions for use in every situation and you can adjust them as you will and as your game develops. The idea is to get started so that you can play the game as soon as possible. Learn by doing.

There are really only 4 or 5 fundamental strokes to learn and you may already have some of these skills from other games you have played.

The serve starts every point. The groundstrokes, forehand and backhand, are used primarily for returning serve and anything in the backcourt. The overhead is used to put away high balls. The volley, of course, is used at the net (kitchen area) when the ball is hit in the air without a bounce. Then there is the dink! Dink, dink, dink! Master the dink more than any other shot. It will improve your game immensely and endear you to any partner with whom you play.

"I love the competition. At my age there are very few sports in which I can play competitively."
-- Steve Riding, age 72, 4.0 level

Serve. The serve can be fancy or plain. It doesn't matter. It only matters that you get it in the court.

Serving a "fault" is the worst of all sins in pickleball. Being limited to only one ball, it is best to keep the serve simple. The simplest serve motion looks somewhat like the motion used in bowling. It is an underhand motion. Swing the arm back below the waist, and then swing it forward, tossing or dropping the ball in front of you to hit. The ball can either bounce before the hit or not, your choice. The ball must be met below a player's bellybutton; however, I've never seen an official check on this rule. Be sure to aim deep and practice a serve that flies safely over the net. Also practice one that is lobbed high over the net. Might as well have some variety. Just make it deep.

Groundstrokes. The groundstrokes – forehand and backhand – should be accomplished with motions that are low to high. It doesn't matter if you start with a loop or a simple, straight back motion. Just bring the paddle forward from low to high so that when you hit the ball it clears the ever-present net. You'll get the knack.

The most commonly used grips for groundstrokes are typical tennis grips without venturing into the extreme western grip some tennis players use with the hand turned well under the handle. To make it easy on the forehand, put your open hand on the paddle handle on the same plane as the face of the paddle before gripping. For the backhand, rotate your hand to the left until your first knuckle is near the top of the handle. Grips are something you have to move around and get a sense of for yourself. These are starting points.

Volley. The volley is a stroke that should remind you of something you must do with all strokes – keep the paddle in front of you! Stand with your feet apart. Your arms should be outstretched a bit, elbows bent, and the paddle in front of you, chin high. The volley stroke is similar to the push motions you see in ping pong, where the wrist leads the hand slightly. Quick blocks and pushes, no swinging necessary, unless the approaching shot is high and tempting. Then, whack it!

I've found that a continental grip is very effective for the volley. That is where the first knuckle on your hand, for a right-hander, is at about 2 o'clock on your paddle's handle. It allows you to hit either a forehand or backhand volley with the same grip. Again, speed is the name of the game. No time to change grips. Hold that paddle in front of you ready for action… and there will be action guaranteed.

Overhead and Lob. The overhead smash is the most delicious shot you can hit in pickleball. It is a sure winner if done correctly. When a high ball is lofted in your direction, raise your arm up and in front of you, and then with your paddle, swat it like a fly and follow through. It can be aimed right, left, middle, deep or short on the court.

On the other hand, if you choose to lob a ball, get out of the way of what is to follow. A lob must be used sparingly, unless you have a very short opponent and a very accurate lob.

Half-Volley. Tennis players know about the half-volley. They instinctively know how to hit it. It is part of that sport's necessary shots. In pickleball it operates the same way. This shot is hit just as the ball touches the court and is on its way up on the rise. It can be hit from a groundstroke position or a dink position in the kitchen. It is absolutely a skill you will need in your arsenal. It is often used offensively as well as defensively. How offensively? It is a quick shot, often hit when your opponent is not ready for it. Or, it can be used as a soft dink. How defensively? Many times your opponents' target will be to hit the ball at your feet. It may be the only shot you can use to stay in a point.

The simplest way to hit the half-volley is to place your paddle just behind the place where the ball is going to land on the court. Then lift the ball up with an open paddle face, high enough to clear the net.

So, do give some time in your practice sessions to the half-volley. When you play a match, you'll be glad you did.

"I was a tennis player. When we moved to Colorado five years ago we tried pickleball. I loved it so much I haven't picked up a tennis racket since!"
-- Nanette Muno, age 64, 5.0 level

Dink. Next, the dink. Dink, dink, dink. Love the dink. Look forward to the dink. Practice the dink until you drop. It uses very simple motions on your forehand, backhand, and even up the middle. The most advice I can give in this area is to always dink in front of you with a soft hand and light grip. Let the head of the paddle drop as you lift the ball over the net. Try to hit the underside of the ball. Easier said than done. But like keeping score, you will get it and eventually be able to dink to your heart's content.

Keep in mind that your opponent may also be dinking to you. Back and forth these delicate rallies go, until someone hits a ball just a bit too high and a slam put-away is inevitable.

Once you have these basic motions down, you can add a few spins and slices that seem appropriate. However, if you are a beginner, stick with the basics until these are mastered.

More Things to Know

There always seem to be more things to learn in pickleball. As soon as you have mastered one aspect of the game, for instance the third-shot drop, there will be another shot to conquer. This is good. This is challenging and it's fun. It's a growing sport. As you grow in it, it grows on you.

Strategy. As you see from what I've already mentioned, strategy pretty much takes care of itself. Get to the kitchen. Lure your opponent into a dink fest. Pounce on any ball that rises above the net and put it away. And too, like most racket sports, if you have a chance, put the ball where your opponents are not!

There are other more subtle strategies, like stacking, which you will learn as you play along. Best to stick with the basics. They are complicated enough!

"Pickleball requires one to calculate angles and velocity faster than your opponents or be extremely lucky. Placement is more important than power or strength. Experience may serve you as much as talent or bravado. So too, men do not have much advantage over skillful women, and age can play with youth, and size is less important than having excuses ready when you miss-hit. Scoring is tough as it goes by ones rather than touchdowns or baskets. Happily, celebratory dancing is encouraged."

    -- Michael "Pancake" Chaussee, age 60-70,
      3.0-4.0 level

Players. The beauty of this game is that you can always find someone weaker than you to play with as well as someone stronger than you. The players whom I have been around are more than gracious to play with less accomplished players, as long as the margin is not too great. And they are full of helpful suggestions, advising on the score, where you should be on the court (usually at the kitchen), and words of encouragement. It seems to be part of the game – helping others understand it and play it better.

On a weekend or holiday, it is a lovely sight to see a park's pickleball courts filled with happy, active people, bouncing around in colorful garb, swinging paddles and sailing balls in every direction. It looks like a Seurat painting with movement. So very festive!

"I love pickleball because it is the best healthy aging activity on the planet!"
Robin Stieber, age 67, 4.5 level

Paddle tapping. This appears to be inherent in the game. It is like the chest bump used in other sports or a new form of "high five." It is customary to paddle tap with your partner when you win a point. Definitely this gesture is shared with all four players at net when a game is finished, win or lose. Join in: it won't hurt your paddle.

Calling lines. Calling lines is the responsibility of every player on the court. You must pay attention to the serves that come to your partner. In turn, your partner must help call the serves that come to you.

Each team is responsible for the calls on their side of the court. If there is a dispute, be sure to make the call in your opponents' favor. That's the gracious thing to do.

"Wherever kindness exists, a happy heart is found."

Ducking. Another important maneuver to develop in rounding out your game is the "duck." Be aware of the length of the court and the speed of a ball and learn to duck when a ball is going to sail out. It is amazing how many points can be won this way. Over-eager tennis players often over-hit pickleballs by miss-judging the length of the court. Duck and say, "Thank you!" when a ball is headed out of bounds.

Shot Selection. When in doubt, **aim down the middle**. This is a helpful strategy whether it's a serve, service return or a general groundstroke with your opponents at net. Oftentimes the two opposing players get confused, can't decide who should take the ball and lose the point in the process.

Videos. As I have said, the best strokes are those that are compact, simple, and control the ball well. Youtube pickleball coaches are plentiful and knowledgeable. Find one or two who provide information for your level, from beginner to intermediate. It is definitely best to learn consistent, efficient strokes from the beginning.

The truth is, it comes down to hitting that wiffle ball again and again in the most appropriate way – sometimes softly and sometimes powerfully. It is about feel and the only way to get it is to do it. This you will learn by touching and carrying or pushing the ball in the manner that is needed. The more you play, the more you will understand what is appropriate and gain this skill. Every ball hit adds to your experience. Miss a few or miss a lot. Adjust as needed.

Skills and Drills. I have found it fascinating that players of all levels are intent on improving their games. They don't just play games or matches; they drill. In the process, their skills improve. Good drills are easy to find. Again, poke through the pickleball Youtube videos on drills and you will be able to find the best ones for you. Be sure to pick ones that cover all of your strokes and movement. It is fun to drill and it's fun to improve!

Balance. Balance is something we all need to have on and off the court, but none more so than seniors. Balance is a challenge, weighing this against that. How much food should one eat? How much water is needed? How much exercise is beneficial? How much rest is required?

As seniors or those close to being seniors, balance is essential in our lives. Oftentimes, we must step back from what we did when we were younger to what is important to do now and not hold any illusions of grandeur, if we ever had them. Even the idea of great accomplishments must be toned down. Life is about enjoying what we are doing at any moment, even when that moment is on a pickleball court.

Life gives and it takes back. As life takes back elements from our physical bodies as we age, like muscle tone, bone mass, and hormones, we must make adjustments. This is one of the beautiful things about pickleball; we can play and enjoy it at any level.
The paddle is light, the court is small and there is very little impact on the arm from hitting a wiffle ball. However, there are a couple of things you can do to help maintain your balance as you move around the court.

Most importantly, **keep your feet under you!** When you are waiting for the ball, use a somewhat wide stance with slightly bent knees. This lowers your center of gravity. Then, when you move toward a ball, do so with your feet, rather than just leaning.

Another helpful hint, is to lower your expectations. When you are learning something new, you miss a lot of balls. Enjoy the delight of simply being able to hit the ball over the net now and then. The sound of the ball popping from one paddle to another can be music to your ears. What an enchanting cacophony it is when you are among 16 courts with balls pinging and popping everywhere!

Warm up a bit before you play. Loosen your arms, move you feet, shake your body, stretch. Control your enthusiasm: be eager, but not too eager, happy but not zealous – balanced!

"Outer balance affects inner balance and vice versa. May we be smart enough to seek it and strong enough to maintain it."

Focus. It goes without saying that the ball should be your focus when playing. It is amazing how often your focus can shift from the ball to the other side of the net or to your opponents or to your business or family elsewhere. Keep it on the ball with a soft focus on the rest of the court, including the position of your opponents. If you should miss a ball, try to figure out where your focus was. You might be surprised at how often it is not on the ball!

At the end of this book is a powerful concentration exercise that you might want to try. It will not only help you focus on the ball when you are on the pickleball court, but it will help you concentrate and problem-solve anything else in your life.

Warnings and Precautions

Safety First. Never, never ever reach behind you for an overhead ball. Smash it if it is in front of you. Or, turn sideways and move back carefully to see it better and position yourself in order to hit it properly.

Never, never try to be a hero and dive for a ball. It is commonly known that people don't bounce, balls do. It is also commonly known that there are more pickleball accidents that end up in emergency rooms than from any other sport. Is it because many of the players of this fine sport have not led sporting lives and are out of shape? Or, is it just that there are more of us out there than those playing other sports?

Addiction! Let it be known that pickleball is absolutely addictive. Women have deserted their families and replaced those household demands with hours on a pickleball court. Men have lost their jobs for nothing more than abandoning their duties for pickleball activities. Teens have been known to skip classes and even interact with seniors in gracious ways on pickleball courts. Seniors and super-seniors are getting in shape and leaving nursing homes and their caregivers. Again, pickleball is the culprit!

Why? My suspicion, which is not backed by science, is that there is always lurking within every player a belief that he or she can play better with every passing game; therefore, the more games the better. When one game is finished, I find myself eager for another. And, **It's Fun! Fun! Fun!**

"If you're not having fun, you're not playing this game right!"

Benefits

Pickleball is a game full of surprises and unintended consequences. It is a game full of possibilities and movement. Move the body and you will oxygenate the blood. Oxygenate the blood and you will lift the spirit. Yes, it is a God-thing! The more you play, the better you feel physically, mentally, and emotionally. Of course, when you feel better yourself, you feel better about everyone and everything else. It is a heart-warming and heart-expanding activity.

Whether a pickleball game is played outside or inside, on a regular pickleball court or a tennis court, it is a healthy recreation.

It is definitely a very social activity. After only a few visits to one of our local pickleball parks, my name and level of play were known by most all of the players. I am now invited to fill in on games when I don't have one scheduled, or practice some drills with one or two other players. The game is welcoming. Conversations are started and friends are made.

I see couples arrive with lunches packed, jugs of water in tow, and a folding chair or two. They are prepared for a morning or even a day of pickleball. They greet their friends and any visitors to the area who might drop in. I have found that people on business trips are now travelling with their pickleball paddles as they can easily find local parks where they can join in the play. No one is ever left out.

"As a recent widow, and an empty nester, there is nothing like pickleball for making new friends, and having fun while exercising. If you don't take it too seriously, there is plenty of time for socializing."
-- Mary Kelley, age 63, 2.5 or maybe 2.0 level

Conclusion

As you can see after reading this book, there is every good reason for you to try pickleball, if you haven't already. It is a healthy, happy game where friends are made and tensions released. In troubling times, you can always count on a pickleball game to lift your spirits. It is a game of inclusiveness in all ways. No size, shape, color, sexual orientation, or economic status defines players.

We, who play this game, love this game. I invite you to join in. Paddle up and paddle on. Get your toe wet and **DARE TO DINK**!

"It's what you do, not what you get that makes you happy."

*****

CONCENTRATION EXERCISE

A mystic gave this Egyptian Yoga exercise to me long ago. It is an exercise that creates new pathways in the brain for more creative thinking. Most of our lives and thinking are ruled by habit, even within the games we play. By giving energy to new areas, new insights are revealed, greater understanding is achieved, and better strategies evolve. These are just a few of the benefits. The rest are for you to discover.

Although the exercise is apparently simple, the effect can be quite powerful. On the other hand, it is wise to avoid expectations.

The intent of the exercise is *clear-sightedness* and will help you see problems more clearly in order to solve them, whether you are on a pickleball court or not. It will also help you focus on the ball with greater ease. I encourage you to give it a try. The effects are quite rapid. The exercise only takes three minutes. It is best to do it several times a day, prior to meals.

Proper Posture

1. Choose a quiet room where you will not be disturbed, preferably with a simple colored wall.

2. Place a small circle, about the size of a penny, on the wall. I've created one above that you can cut out and attach with tape. Or, you may get a felt one at any hardware store.

Place the circle or dot on the wall at exactly eye level when you are seated, and about four to seven feet away from you. During the exercise, "rest" your eyes on this dot without "staring" and without blinking. If there is a source of light in the room, it should be behind you.

3. Sit on a chair with your back straight, not touching the back of the chair. Place your feet flat on the floor, heels about two inches apart, legs and knees open, forming a V shape with the feet and legs.

4. Adjust the height of the chair seat so that your thighs are exactly parallel to the floor and form a right angle to the rest of your body. Straighten your spine, keeping your shoulders slightly pulled back and your chin in.

5. Rest your hands on your thighs, just behind the knees so that the thumbs will point to the inside of the knees, while the fingers, spread open, point to the outside. They should also form a V.

6. Draw your abdomen in gently. Keep your lips lightly closed with your tongue relaxed, resting on the bottom of your mouth, and your teeth slightly parted.

7. Relax every muscle in your body except for those that hold your spine straight.

Preparatory Breath

The purpose of the preparatory breath is to clean the lungs. It consists of a rapid breath made up of short inhalations and expirations through your nose, one after the other without a pause. After seven or eight of these rapid breathing cycles, end with a long and forceful exhalation through your mouth, expelling as completely as possible all the stale air from your lungs.

The Exercise

The exercise is based on the seven-plus-one second rhythm. It would be ideal to use your heartbeats instead of seconds as the units of time. With a little practice you will be able to sense this time interval as a musical beat, without paying much attention to it. (**For children**, a five-plus-one second rhythm might be more appropriate.)

Check your posture. Make sure you are relaxed. Make the preparatory breath, then "rest" your eyes on the dot, almost as if you are looking through it to infinity.

***

Breathe in for seven seconds (or seven heartbeats), hold your breath for one second, breathe out for seven seconds, keeping the lungs empty for one second. This makes <u>One Breath Cycle</u>. You will do this twelve times.

***

As you inhale, visualize a spiral of "energy" coming into the very center of you clockwise in seven concentric circles. During the exhalation, unwind the spiral counter-clockwise from the center of you outward in seven increasingly larger circles. Do not localize either the very center of yourself or the spiral. Try to "feel" its sweeping movement as you would "feel" a tornado, if you were the atmosphere. Every motion (or energy) in the Universe has the form of a spiral, therefore this visualizing-feeling will attune you to the universal form of motion.

<u>If you blink during the exercise, start again!</u>

After you have gotten the hang of this part of the exercise and have become fairly familiar with it, and NOT before, you may complete the exercise as follows.

During the first three breath cycles (remember a cycle consists of seven counts in, hold for one, and seven counts out, hold for one) imagine that the dot on the wall is red, while at the same time a red light illuminates the abdomen, sexual area of the body, and the back of the head.

During the next three breath cycles, imagine the dot to become yellow, while at the same time a yellow light bathes your chest area and your forehead.

For the next three cycles, imagine the dot becoming blue (cyan blue) and a blue light illuminating your solar plexus and the top of your head.

Finally, during the last three breaths, imagine the dot becoming white with a brilliant white light illuminating your face, arms and legs.

That is the complete exercise.

***

When you have mastered this exercise, you definitely deserve a trophy, or at least another round of pickleball! Have fun! Play happy! The happier you are, the better you play!

***

There are associations or clubs that promote the sport of pickleball in nearly every town now. They offer information on lessons, sites, round-robins, tournaments, and more. Mine is the Pikes Peak Pickleball Association. The USA Pickleball Association is the national governing body that provides guidelines for the sport.

About the Author/Illustrator

Sally Huss was a National and Wimbledon Junior Champion, a Wimbledon semi-finalist in singles and doubles, winner of many National senior singles and doubles titles, and still plays ladies league tennis on occasion! She is a newcomer to pickleball and has found it to be a great addition to her life.

"Bright and happy," "light and whimsical" have been the catch phrases attached to the writings and art of Sally Huss for over 40 years. From inspirational books, children's books (over 100 and counting) to her King Features syndicated newspaper panel "Happy Musings," all of her creations are happy in nature and free-spirited in style.

Sally is a graduate of USC with a degree in Fine Art and through the years has had 26 of her own licensed art galleries throughout the world.

To view Sally's other books and art, go to: www.sallyhuss.com

www.ingramcontent.com/pod-product-compliance
Lightning Source LLC
Chambersburg PA
CBHW042218050426
42453CB00001BA/5